Vestigial

Page Hill Starzinger

Winner of the Barrow Street Press Poetry Prize,
selected by Lynn Emanuel

Vestigial

Page Hill Starzinger

Barrow Street Press
New York City

Designed by Robert Drummond
Cover art by Stephen Croeser
        Detail of *Ink on Paper*, 2011
Author photo by Monty

Published by Barrow Street Press
Distributed by:
        Barrow Street Books
        P.O. Box 1558
        Kingston, RI 02881

First Edition

Library of Congress Control Number: 2013938338

ISBN 978-0-9893296-0-6

For David Baker, with love

CONTENTS

IV

Acknowledgments

> *do not Crush*
> *Me all to mammocks:*

—Edward Taylor

I

Collectio

1.

Let's review.
      Which reminds me of a little-known fact. Here
the punctuation hangs,
         the words fall away
with habit. *All hearts be open*
            no secrets hid
     Be with your self.

See
the translucent skin, knotty veins
        of your grandmother.   Inhabited, and
so inhabitable.   If the door

is closed, trouble is nearby,
     the ferryman
        drawls. Through a latticework

of canals flows
     wastewater,
     flushed north
        to irrigate farmland.
     Another Afghan woman sets herself
on fire.   "Surprised Kitty"
is viewed more than 28,500,000 times on YouTube.   *They only scream*
once
     says a high school student who spent 14 days in captivity
        and witnessed dozens of killings.   TAPILI, Congo.
     And with your spirit
you sing.
     On stage,

2.

a baby carriage hurtles
        down a staircase.
                Gravediggers uncover, excavate, bury, then
reverse the process. These, Jewish graves—the work of Muslim, Arab, Palestinian
hands.

And our defense minister says

        there are a lot of kinetic actions taking place
along that border.

                        Pray
tell.   Mother

        walks into a pond,
        grey head disappears, no one reaches her.

Bent, the cage inside is locked;
                no bigger than a

        coffin.

3.

                        Thy Lord

If the story of a great fortune
is a forgotten crime, then
is misfortune a remembered   generosity?

                Give as if they were
        alms.

Settle, as in
Sisyphus.

Shhh, she used to say;

and the prayer flags
fray—.   99

is not 100, a picker at the Brazilian
landfill reminds us.
Unfold your hands,
fall a
part.

Æ

This fissure—constitutive
of the self, not
a cracked self.
A gift
of precisely
what is now refused; a pre-
fix to
crave. *kräfva,*
Da. *kræve* to require,
exact: - conjectured
to be the root of *craft.*
Disputatious
dark energy expanding (*it seems
now that the answer is not
really zero*
[another infinity we grasped,
that moved from sacrilege to hol-
iness]):
they tell us we live only
where life is possible,
just as fish exist exclusively
in water. Or
that we live in a multiverse,
all kinds of universes
and—here's the point:
we search for solutions but
they may come from unchartable lands
in the manner of miracles—
like love. Can you follow
yourself? Unstitch.
Rename as
entropy. Smithson's invisible holes
—from auger borings—
an *alphabet of sites:* you and I,
made for ruin.

Lyms of

Rim of light. Crawling to the black
basalt edge. I'll say the wrong
thing and move in with him. Falls are the river's way
of getting back to normal. Simultaneously a mistake
and correction: in order to erase itself. At the rift between
the water's force and its path. (The physical industry of it.)
What causes the smoke to rise so high
out of water, the Kololo asked. (About Victoria.) So
Leonardo wrote backward, right to left
using the left hand without punctuation. So

limb means border
        all be but lyms of blissidnes
when you face limits
rip them
       off
Sub up to = *limen* lintel
Hee on the wings of cherub rode
        towering. *arch.* and
Errant.
(in quest of
      , or
poet.
9. Astray,
     b. as pred.?
Quantum pop.   Loss

is a second acquisition. When you are preparing:
dig a hole big enough for a friend. Straighten
the top vertebra. In the 1970s Deborah Butterfield made horses
out of mud and sticks, *combined the figure*
and the ground. For half a century the city of light
had candles in only three sites. Now it spends $260,000 a day.
Our insula "lights." How long I ignored it: folded
and tucked deep. It took imaging. The same for the addict:
it is not just. But: heart rate, blood pressure,
tickle in lungs, taste. This is love, baby. Remember

to screw in light bulbs
tightly
      next. With a titbit
on your nose.
Trust,
     trussed.
Baggage.
Cluster or head of.
     with a tie-rod or struts, so as to
8. fasten the wings
or legs of (a
     fowl. before
flight):—O
in a spinning trace
     flanis flew ane felloun

You could say: I'm going to trust myself. And it will become
part of me. Note: Indian giver. In folk tales if you hold on
to a gift you usually die. Sweetness starts
on the tongue but it doesn't end there. The secret is
the democratization of puzzle invention. We like to fill up
empty spaces. In nurikabe—*islands in the stream*—
no isle can touch another. Look for
the most constrained parts (often the corners).
Try to work between. The wall? Impedes.
Extends forever. Knock low to make it disappear.

A Karstic

1.

Tell me your anodyne ways. My heart,
all day, gnawed on. Hobbes.
Find your mumble   hinging

Less on plot.
Buff   cretaceous
Karst.

Karst-land [see BLIND
Etched and eroded
Lost all semblance of normal

A chaos of pits, flutes, runnels   In the past
too much emphasis on solution and on associated collapse

of passages.   Upland of exposed carboniferous limestone

2.

while milkless and childless before you I stand.

Is cá bhfuil mo locht nach dtoghfaí mé roimpi?

3.

corruption of

boireann: barren, stony   Rich with fertile
rock   rainwater seeps & spills into grikes between clints
cavernous karst fenster   cascades into sinkhole   swallowed
by turlough deposited with white marl   under dense sward

of a rare sky-violet, across the shallow silverweed;
at the marsh creeps mint, pondweed, buttercups, knotgrass. Tumble
of rocks, black with bracken, where water fleas and fairy shrimp spawn.
Lacy fan-shaped leaflets on maidenhair spring on shady,

forms loose hummocks, deeply cut, dark, turns crimson near the roost
of horseshoe bats that emit echolocation calls;
yellow meadow ants suckle on honeydew from root aphids

4.

Grief is a process of disassembly

Deforming the given.

97% of our DNA looks like gibberish
The dark matter of inner

Shirr
Shim
Shake and
salt
Yoke   tell me
of gold and gem
which clothe the barren-grounds
Bang on the blue
Rise and flap in gutters
O heap o' shirrels an' peat-mow
how precious the deadness

Aphasia

1.

Blackened birdcage. Torn magnolia petals.
The door, latchless, swings open.
I become your tongue.
51,000 sculptures in honeycombed grottoes:
out of my mouth flies a Chinese bird spider.

Do you know not to catch it in your hand?

Quick, here's Blanchot:
1.   *discover the generosity of disaster*
2.   *ladies and gentlemen") Celan wanted to tell us*

A girl found at Hiroshima was singing to her doll.

Verse b. To impose upon; to cozen, cheat
c. Turning to begin another line

2.

Every good marriage begins in tears, a Kyrgyz saying goes.
Outside were ten men. *The second man pulled her hands away.*

Ala kachuu: grab and run.
Cheaper than paying $800 plus a cow.

Her father says
I'll let him take her. Love comes and goes.

In the heart
of the country is a lake that empties
and then refills: dammed
by a glacier under
which the water drains,
leaving ice in bed.

A land where tribes have roamed, and wild sheep with long horns

Blind   **Blind-story** (Arch.),
            below the clerestory   *blesti* to become dark,
Lettish *blendu* I do not see clearly,   O

3.

the earth cracks open and fires burn in tunnels.
Coal waste stands 500 feet tall: black
sandstorms blow into Shanxi.
            even during the day we drive with lights on."

Husband 600 feet underground. Digging out

the stereo, refrigerator, television, electric fan, phone, light bulbs.

Ms. Cao decorates the family   *with Chinese film stars*
            and three-inch heels

The yellow loess rich
            but eroding the cradle
this, of
Nine-Heaven Palace
Midair Temple
Sacred Mountain
            Flying Stones

Scripture
suspended in shadow,
            as light splays
between letters
            scripturient   of late L.
                        desire   ,**f.L.**   bag for alms

—black tongue.

Þ

Ye olde
        thorn or
giant
among
        the litter:

        voiceless
fricative, mistaken
for archaic
        you;
replaced by
diagraph
        th as in there

        we twine—
fragment of us
ascender:
        windrow. The
scatter I trust,
the trail:
        —within, still

        the promise.
Notes of
nature strung
        by cylindrical
circulation:

can you believe
        they
sing
        like an angel?

II

Remnants

The novel he gave me has
belted kingfishers—*Megaceryle alcyon*—

who plunge into bodies

of water, disappear, emerge. Tiny bits of magnetite
in their skulls steer migrants home to nests across

a hemisphere. Accidentals blown off course.

They live in a flock of a different species:
the problem is, they can't breed.

————

Here I am ripping a seam—strings frayed, smell of
burning plastic. I stand on a rock plinth

stained lilac. This is what we do.

I am going to make
the same soufflé as my mother: sharp

cheddar. Teeth marks. He said, *I like*

the intimate presence of living with a woman.
Shred and tear. There is still

————

a door I can't open. It is stone-grey
steel: rust running in puddles.

I want the man's—his—attention. And can't.

What if there's another? How
many. Who would want to share

this form of absence. He said—porous entry—

there are many caves in Missouri and when you
walk inside *the landscape changes*

———

with every step. Flaking kauri tree, cones with twisted-
winged seed. Spiraling needles of rimu pine

clasped by nocturnal parrot, with whiskers.

The kingfisher beats its fish against a rock, tosses it,
then swallows headfirst. Rattles, and a loud cry.

Ash at the tips of the nails—

Border Land

White phlox—*flame* in Greek—tempted night-moths
with sweetness, its rhizomes crept near fire-
cracker-red bee balm,
this *Jacob,*
whose

propagation is by division:
the cultivar self-seeded but did
not grow true to
the parent. I am
forgetting:

the Iceland poppy: wiry stems, trans-
lucent tissue-paper petals—*all
parts likely to be
poisonous.*
But no worries:

mother gave up on her garden—ours,
where I grew up—and then it
eroded so
slowly no
one noticed:

the steep bank eating the earth (will it
swallow the house in 50 more years?).
I can't remember
the names of
other flowers

or what they looked like.
Call it the angel's share.

———

Strike a match—red phosphorus
converts to white: watch
the tip
blacken.

———

I tell her I think I'll either be sheltered
or homeless. *What is the same in both situations?*
she asks. The self, I say. *You keep
erasing it.*

———

Quiz. Is a mummified tattooed Maori head
A. work of art. B. body part

While you decide: know it was
carved with *uhi* (chisels) to groove and ridge,
darkened with *ngarehu* (burnt timbers) and *awheto*
(caterpillar). Sacred, the heads were
severed. Preserved.

———

At dinner what is left
            are outbursts
                        corroding

———

Earth-scent of burnt wood drifts
near the top of the bank,
a thin line of dried bracken,
bitterwort and devil's horn
rattling. At the door,
on the welcome mat,
a Blue Point Siamese curls up
in shifting light.
She'll be gone
before the chill drops.

Charcoal Suite

1. Scratch

Cedar. Molten silver. Black stumps. Bedroom
door ajar. Fur against inner wall. How

the dogs tear at the soil. The way a map
that shows little can be useful. Straddle

and slap. *Shall my life twine breake.* You hand me
the scissors. My leg slides off the mattress.

Take yourself seriously, you say. Sun
drops into swamp holly. I walk to the back

of your eye. Does it flower? The lit deer
tethered in the front yard. Kiss on stomach.

Scratch of pen. You hit the return key hard.
I imagine a man in the attic

checking floorboards so the squirrel won't fall. Please
don't say *process.* You write, *Dear sleepy.* How

much can you see through a slit? I argue,
just enough. My finger in the crook of your palm.

2. Char

You of two ex-wives. Me of no husband.
The ladder warns: *Keep body centered. Do
not overreach.* I eat her walnut bread.

It's good with sharp cheddar. Did she teach you
that? I am watching you remember her:
a movie I can't catch sight of. But I

smell her: cheese melting on cranberry. Bas-
ket of bittersweet. Deer belly in weeds.
House burnt black: making way for an ex-

pressway. I am taking the USB
memory stick out of your computer.
In the Lévinas you circle, *Hope does*

*not refer like an awaiting, to some
thing that must come about.* Name every
way you have lit a fire.

3. Nest

There is a knocking. Small and distinct. Hand
on bark. Flash of red. Swollen river. I
trail behind. As we drive, rain on windshield,
you don't turn on wipers. *I'm looking past
the drops.* At the gas station, a hole in
the canopy and from it the sound of
small birds. 25¢ coffee. At the

airport, afterward, I head in the wrong
direction. I say, *I really can take
care of myself.* In an e-mail, you say
you are rooting wild holly so we'll have
bushes for our house, wherever that may
be: bending a low branch to the earth, press-
ing it with a rock and letting it be.

4. Land

Watching a fairy tale, I sweat. Cats curl
in a box lined with vermillion. On
the counter, wedge of soft Gorgonzola,
crostini, red peppers. Sweet. When did I

deserve this. Painting of baby ram, on
its side, front and back legs, *hobbled. That is
the wranglers' term,* you write. *Also hog-tied,
but that's just unpoetic.* What makes a

relationship work. Kiki Smith crafts *Black
Eggs,* 1998. Glass with acid
wash. 137 units.
Bring grace to this anxious tableau. I stand

next to you looking at a nude woman,
back flayed. Another pisses jewels on
the floor. Turquoise beaded crotch. Lucio
Fontana calls his cuts *attese,* mean-

ing *wait* or *expectation.* Here are my
scars: inch above nipple. Left toe. Ankle.
Ovary to ovary. In the mid-
dle of the word *intoxication* lies

toxic. I say to a friend, *think of it
as cinema.* The stuff in between the
bones. To move and be elastic. To leap.
To land when you fall. Is it possible

we are unbreakable. Is it deep spring.
We can draw cuts. A new world. A tower.
This is our cutting. No baby. No
nursery. Pigeon alights across the street.

Unaccounted for

You: there——: everything behind us swings back-
ward, and everything before

opens outward. What a wonderful sunny ward
you populate: within it, the earth-chocolate

breath of the fuchsia-pistilated *Oncidium*——
and the slivery aphrodisiac-

al pods of Vanillin: all, now missing. How
can I thank you?—I have found nothing

as confounding
to their carefully constructed

plot——
as you!: You——

won't disappear:
what is that?: pouf: that's how it goes.

Did no one teach you that? Here,
let me try. I am the mother of

the disappeared: *los desaparecidos.* Just look for me
around any corner. My arms——open.

III

Reduction

Vestigial *leavinges*
and fragmentes.
These. However: whole—
    like us
a piecing together;

        recovered
—*or a kind of gluing,*
like dinosaurs from Hell Creek Formation,
with soft tissue and blood vessels inside
        femurs.

Recursive
is not the point, not even
Chomsky's theory—embedding entities
within like entities—a tree structure.
Because the most powerful ancient

Amazon cultures, who resist
change, have no stories
for what came before. There, prosody—present tense:
woman winding raw
cotton, child at her feet, singing

a series of notes,
like a muted horn (what
sounds).
        What

is not enough about this? Could we fall prey

to transcendence,
and reduce, to a point that is
fugitive; you are at the tip

of my tongue, then
not. Just like a leaf drifting
out of the picture. It's called

xibipio—
not simply gone,
but out of experience. Of Christ
they ask: have you met
      him?

Old Habits

If change is a matter of catching

ourselves—taking *three conscious breaths,*
what about redwoods falling,
        breaking

canopy,
letting light in so saplings spring—a phenomenon called
        release?

In that second
        are we finally found?—only if we are there?—
I mean

here.

As if *Intifada*—which literally means
        shaking off,
also,
        uprising—
is only a concept.
        During the Second *Intifada,*

on the West Bank, 500,000 olive trees
        bulldozed, burnt—uprooted:

Abu Awad wraps the

stumps in

sackcloth.
Goat's covering: cilice.

Fundamentally,
a discomfort.

      Think of the peacock
who eats poison
      and his feathers
      become more
      brilliant.

Shenpa is what Buddhists
      call it, stuck—literally *attachment.* Also
hooked:

think of the marbled murrelet—
      small seabird *associating with upwellings*—

it lays a single egg in crowns of coastal conifers

endangered now,
where I find myself: old growth. Harder to
revise the narrative—but

an aerie

of bark

      and heartwood. One way to see it:
      —do not cause harm.

Knock, Knock

1.

Who's
there? Me. But some bifurcation early on
makes the sense of
    yours truly
unseen, indistinct, fleeting . . .
      foremelting
      (don't you like that: 1606 antecedent for
invisible).

         Can you challenge that pattern?

         If I'm paying you all the money, can't you fix it.

2.

Meanwhile, in Delhi, 60% live
    in makeshift homes
  without clean water.
      In Japan,
    the Paper Church and Curtain House
    are *loved.*

Anopticall.
1598. *Obs.*   *Not in the field of vision.*

         Reminds me of apocryphal.

         It's being able to claim what you need

3.

                              Listen up: dread is running
braided down my damp back.
        A lash of black catkins
rooting in a cypress swamp.

                Try to connect rather than split

                Part takes comfort, part is dismayed

                Don't make it mysterious.

Ah, just a
                shift in consciousness. I
have allies (fragments—my
        specialty) and *Wisdom of
No Escape*, dog-eared. But it's a long time
until the next
out-breath.

4.

Design me
a burrow built-in
        with loss. Order-to-measure. Snow
        packed.
Icicles! Dripping. Sun, view of stars. Pack of dogs—the 5,000 euthanized every
day, one every 16 seconds: rescue the buggers.

                What's familiar is sadly not disappearing.

                Even one tiny diamond, I say.

Think of it not as deprivation, but as gift.

Eucharist Nervosa

Diet of brittle wafer. Blood boxed tight.
Boxcar motherland. How it
shimmers: the throne. On cheap typewriter paper,
thank you, she writes, *for telling me.* Did you
say ash? A man in an Irish kilt pushes a woman
in a wheelchair. The cemetery used to be
a ski slope with a lodge instead of a morgue.
Father is walking in circles looking for
family. Blue Jay, old pine, lichen on
empty birdhouse. Open the back and there's
a dead wasp. And the call on my cell—
static. There is not asking, not
answering, not telling: mother calls it fun & games.
At night I hear icicles slide off the roof. The name
of the stream twisting in its bed
is Blood Brook. Thin slip of ice on inlet,
clotted white at shore. 300 British toy soldiers
boxed in his closet. On the wall
hangs *Starving Letters:* seven drawings
created by snails eating through Chinese rice
paper. *Carta Famina,* the title
means map and letter. Remember Galileo,
the master of falling bodies, died
blind. Under house arrest.

Terroir

1. Unshelter

I can't open the door and even if I draw a doormat
on the floor, I can't break out. Keep low: underneath,

I see the sill, my slice of. Thin enough for a Cantor's turtle
—no shell—which spends its life motionless, buried

in sand, surfacing twice a day for one breath each. I
could whittle myself into fiction. Sol

LeWitt's breakthrough wall drawings—sketched
from ceiling to floor—like modern cave art

—are made to be painted over. What is
left behind? LeWitt sketched diagrams. The turtle lays eggs. Me?—

the Chinese would say, *swallow nesting on a curtain.*
In L.A.: set of box springs

on freeway shoulder. Man says, unshelter oneself.
Don't limit oneself to *words* when there are *sentences.*

2. Cast-Off

The hummingbird sings outside your office
—little quick chirps—

like a chipmunk. This delights you.
Louise Nevelson, in *Dawn's Wedding Feast,* 1959:

painted stacked wooden crates filled with street finds—
shutters, hubs, chess pieces—all-white. Absolved. And you,

who see: the jambs, the archvolt, the panic bar,
the peephole. You put your fingers on my right arm and said

I'll find you.

3. Outland

I'd like to spend a weekend not thinking about it.
Don't tell me *it's about befriending who we are already.*

I repainted the closet, threw out what was inside.
What do you give up when you're a prisoner.

You lie down in the dirt. *Wise people,* says
a *New York Times* reporter, quoting one, C.,

a 67-year-old mother of seven (seven?), *don't sit
around and dwell.* California spends in excess

of $55 million on litter removal. Fresh Kills Landfill
in Staten Island is one of two man-made structures

you can see from space. The other? Great Wall of
China. The Greeks got it right: they named

the seahorse-shaped hippocampus—where memories
lie—*sea monster.*

Alpha Protein

1.

In the world of gift
      you can't have your cake
              unless you eat it.   —Hyde)

Helix

      a curve on any
developable surface
    screw

as long as preload
      is not exceeded,
bolts will not   come loose

2.

ABIDJAN, Ivory Coast, August 19—
    Toxic cocktail   laced with
dumped in

by Greek-owned tanker   Panamanian flag
      leased by the London   branch of
          a Swiss   with a fiscal in

high concentrations   *you can no longer smell*
      because it paralyzes
        your nervous system

this, in a republic
    boasting a full-size replica of St Peter's in Rome
consecrated by the Pope

gift *bestowed* but   *At present,* travel
    is *ill-advised.* Police *can be excitable*
armed elements are

under influence of   Keys to the economy:
          oil industry and
active chemical industry   specializing in lubricants

3.

When it moves in a circle   each gift
          is an act of faith.   Beyond the *private skin*
and in its final

          expansion no body at all.

4.

NELAMANGALA, India—
          Crossing the Broken Boat River
5 million truck drivers   buy

sex several times a day   rarely using condoms
          exposing their wives   and future children
                    half of all

blood bought   from poor
          30 percent   not
tested

my astrologer
          says I'm going to die anyway at 40
of course the girls want to use condoms   *only pretty ones*

can be choosy

Gift   Old High German,
                    commonly *gif,* poison),
                            Old English, str. Fem. (recorded only in the sense
        'payment for wife'

Screw   simple
                    machine used to
        translate torque into linear force   *the mating helix (taps and dies*

5.

MT. WASHINGTON, KY July 2004—
            prankster posing as police officer—over the phone—
instructs assistant manager at McDonald's

to strip-search a teenage employee
            By the end of the evening the caller had also persuaded
                The manager's fiancé to abuse

at least 70 other people   DNA is
                helical and many proteins   known
                            as alpha helices while

Helix is also
            the outer rim of the ear,
                        collecting sound   acting
        as a funnel, amplifying   sometimes has
            a kink

Loosestrife

—another aggressive foreign invader,
dainty, like milfoil, with tiny four-
petaled white blooms, stems whorled
by feathery leaves which tangle in
limbs and propellers. Who knew the aquarium

was such a source of evil. In Cairo,
the *fatwa* declares an unmarried man
and woman can work together if she
breast-feeds him five times, *to establish family
ties.*

       ———

        Carrion in the road.   Wings lifting.
Devil's
        ditch.   No wonder
          we learn to bend
light the wrong
        way to render   invisible.
Stud
        the skull
         with 8,601 diamonds
—sell it for $100 million.

       ———

Meanwhile, in southern Sudan after 25 years
of civil war, aerial surveys reveal herds
rivaling those of the Serengeti: 1.3 million
gazelles, kob and tiang, in a single 30-by-50-
mile column migrating across savannas. No zebra,

the reporter notes. We look
for the single error, line by line,
like pickup sticks. Or: the disguising
euphemism for half an ounce of lead entering
a man at great velocity. It doesn't fit.

Riptide

INDIANAPOLIS, I.L., OCT. 26—
Body of sixteen-year-old.
More than 150 burns, bruises, sores, cuts and scaldings.
I'm a prostitute and proud of it carved into left abdomen.
      Torture had been communal by assorted

Short cut, a crossing
            Also **near cut.**   to heaven from every place
                  disfigure (
                        To carve (a peacock

dis'flesh, v. b. To free from
      disembody.

BAMIYAN, Afghanistan—
Empty niches that once held colossal Buddhas
now gape in the rock face—
        explosives at the base and the shoulders blew them
             great scar marks the inner
                a silent cry at the

self
    obscure
        Mining. Of a rock, etc.: Detached,
            they are   self-stones.

how we allow it.

Crutch. Or is it

Death is like a return of being in itself.
An irreducible or privileged relationship.

to possess. To

pick until it bleeds. Opening to what's.
light.
bare stripping. To
locate.
      the riptide

How memories lodge and you have to peel them back.

Then stand in the spaces.
      Thus the rituals

sterile dermal needles. Large kitchen matches.
Low buzz running between pins.
Mugwort smolders at tip
The *gating* of pain

EGG HARBOR TOWNSHIP, N.J., NOV. 21—
Each barefoot.
Each facedown in several inches of water, head tilted to the east.
Four prostitutes in a drainage ditch behind a strip of motels
He can relive his fantasy through the shoes
which serve as trophy

there is the night we were in the closet
and I closed the door

or was that you

—it's called *a screen memory*

In the mountain cloud forest of Ecuador
a rare vampire
has a tongue
that stretches up to three times its length
to reach the sweet nectar
in the corolla

20. A turning aside, a deviation; also.

Ruskin's model of *divine proportion*

mourning,
        Where the subject does not know what has been lost

Arachne

I wash my hands. In the gallery, a green soap bicycle lies beside a bronze bucket of
water *suggesting the potential for erasure.* I wash
my hands. The Uighurs harvest jade from the muddy Yorungqash river, polished
smooth, *medicinal and even magical.*

      Flowing from the biblical site of the Garden of Eden, the Shatt Al Arab is
drained, diverted and fetid, not reaching the Persian Gulf.
      From God, it comes. I wash my
hands.

Here's a riddle: Each night we lose it and each morning it comes back.

And yet, on top of the Verrazano, a 4,260-foot double-decker suspension bridge,
      a family of peregrine falcons relocates to a nest
built by the Metropolitan Transportation Authority,
         high above the tidal straits
sculpted during the last ice age. The Lenape paddled
out to meet the explorer. Matrilineal, the tribe,
calling their primary crops The Three Sisters: beans, to climb up the maize,
and squash to spread along the ground, preventing weeds.

I keep trying to shape a story. I keep disappearing. It suits others,

sometimes. Why wouldn't it. In Madagascar,
we take ancestors from their tombs for a party, *famadihana*—
        dancing with the dead, then laying the bundled corpses
on the ground, reshaping them so they look more human. *The bones
     are valuable to us and must never be
lost.* Meanwhile we can't read the names
on the shrouds, the ink fades.
Maybe

it doesn't matter. I still have three small eggs attached

to one fluid-filled follicle. Don't tell me
      when they   disappear.

I like to think, now: history repeats itself. A terminal   is both end
     —and beginning.
              A map locates   or loses.   Make like a spider:
            Grasp and scamper
   on the skeins, tiny claws and
         hairs at tips of legs to
hang upside down.   Sewing silk-lined burrows
  with tripwires and trap
                doors.   I wash
    my hands.   I wash my body. I plunge

into it.

IV

Corpse Flower

Of what you left in the dark, and never saw.
Of what you thought might hang in the tree, but never touched.
A mossy velvet damp: fecund, but also somehow, at the same time,
    shiny and specular, hard like metal,
precious like platinum, no, more like diamonds, deep blue. Tag,

you're it.

A razor-thin man standing guard
        cradles an electric saw,
fleet of gnomes at his feet
                clutching leashes to miniature
Doberman pinschers,
mouths snapped shut, ready to spring. You walk by
but never away, watching
        a girl, jettisoned, at a Chinese train station,
        Picasso asking Marie-Thérèse to be his wife (after he found
a new mistress). If only you

could tap her round

shoulders. And down from the heavens,
crystalline hail pelts as sun scatters among the pour.
Unfolding at once, thousands of bloodred flowers
    leaping out of split leaves from *Amorphophallus titanum,*
fragrant like carrion, as warm as a human body, obsession of flesh flies.

Poultice

1.

Such is the pulse

at the table under the conversation.
Whorled. A spike driven beneath lids
and swirled like an eggbeater. Turtles
might live indefinitely—turning their hearts
off and on at will—if humans didn't crush them.

At the top of the stair: curled. Shut
doors. Wall full of mice. Thalamus
means *bedroom chamber*. Inside:
a rustling of twigs and
bird in the arches. Wings against stone.

I cannot uproot you so completely, you say.
I tell you: transplants
need containers approximately
twice the size. Be sure the spade is sharp
so cuts heal rapidly. Water to settle disturbed soil.

There is the smell again. Mother in bed drinking martinis.

2.

I lay down in the bottom of the birds' nest and count my feathers. 10,000 mites,
200 gnats. Scabious. Can't see the ground. A world in a cup. Airplane vapor
       for clouds.
Nest is a bed. Fetal on feathers. Empty mattress.
A stilt palm grows roots out of a stem that angles to the earth.

3.

If there's nowhere to hide, set out to have a deaf child.

Labradoodle.

The fields look hungry, I say.
That's because you're living in New York,
you say.

Puzzlingly useless object. The project is to comprehend
the continuing opaqueness.

      [Centaur vi *Men in themselves opaque, who borrow beams*

Take Reverón: dressing life-size dolls
like models. Pink lip gloss. Chills! Dig up tin crown. Sell to MoMA.
Color spit-bite with flat-bite. Care
for a Chihuahua with a blue hue?
Or a purse-size poodle. Some lack
eyes and a nose. Others are so severely
brain damaged they run in circles all day.

Dr. Bob said it took him 17 years to marry his wife. My father
rowed the same stretch of the Connecticut 10,105 times. My brother
circumnavigated the globe twice. This is not a competition. Oh no.

There's no way you can piece it back—just
cover the barren and nicked
stem. Pin it.

Tiger on limb flicking.

As I approach the door, I see a mirror on the back.

Three sticks of dynamite to my chest. Next time
you touch me you're going to blow your hand off.

Erasure

You've been living, she says, *as if you don't
really count.* Cerebral minimalism comes to mind.
*As if, in your psychology, there is no acknowledgement
of the future.* The Overhand Bend knot (a.k.a. Euro
Death Knot) joins two splayed ropes. The bitter
ends emerge on the same side: it is prone
to catastrophic failure. Also used for shopping tag-
strings. *Swapper Day* reads the sign on the highway

to the gorge. The trouble is overdue: count
the characters. Crossed-wedded silt and shale,
as if cemented, the streambed forces water down,
carving Black Hand sandstone—fluvial sediment,
clasts of the underlying—and plunges,
legend has it, to Hades. Hanging from the lip,
young hemlocks dangle from webs of roots, like dream-
catchers. Tall fissured pines spread Medusa-roots

back from the edge. *I wonder what it's like to hear them fall.*
They are falling now, you say, *all the time.* In the movie
everyone chases an object with no relation to the plot.
As if pursuing something else is truer than accepting
what's here. *Erasure*—from *arace*—first meant uproot. Just
give me my thighbone, my ragged teeth, and cut off
my hair: I'll weave a tear-shaped charm to filter
what grows in our darkest earth. Night. Fury. Claws.

Blue Moon

Woad—

the indigo drips from
        our fingers,
                converted to white
                reverting to insoluble blue, but still
fugitive

& between the emerging spirals of crystal and mud
        jutting
                from bloodred
                waters, silt accumulates
foreign to the piece

but inherent to the work—
        gone
                in ten years or one;
                this is, we think, what
he wanted—

and somewhere between moon and sky
        you lean
                over and kiss
                the top of my head,
unscrolling

the illuminated
                rice paper parchment,
                    handing me
                    the india ink
compounded

from soot, pine smoke,
        lamp oil, musk
                and donkey skin,
                waiting
as if nothing lost could not be found—

Seepage

Listen: puddles, rubbed-in stains,
chewing gum ground into tarmac,
scratched CDs,
glitches printing a document through the feeder at an odd angle.
What
would you ask if you could?
Stammer
of pavement apparitions. Recall the superintendent
from Chile, who brought his penguin to the city. A gentleman
kissing like butterfly wings—*effleurer*. But
do not pluck
a feather for your phrase:
my father dreamed
he could walk backward
through his life, see what he missed. Or
return as Mallory to re-climb Everest (what of the
puncture?).
How would you build your memory palace:
is it ice. Vapor. Charred wood.
Pay attention to
the shadow falling out of your teacup.
Finger
the clock. Binoculars.
Enter the barrel from behind the peak
of the breaking wave: hollowness—then, your choice.

How to save it?

Squander

I want to squander you. Headstrong
into hummocks under rowan
and alder. With **lust.** after WANDER. Hence
maniac. Right and left
inclose the rear; DESIDERIUM.
So greedy lookes of yong. To be
d. simply. Holy Thistle. Spine and
prickle. The Stuart Queen embroidered *In my end
is my beginning.* Rooted not so much
in barren, as in good ground
uncared for: neglected.

Carduus, Carlina, Cardoon, Saltwort, Blessed.

Her head fell out of its wig. A dog
rushed out of her skirts. Liturgical
color of martyrdom. Purple-pink
inflorescence globe-shaped with florets (disc
and ray). Tipped with pappus
of slender bristles. From Greek *acanthus,
perdo* and *onos:* meaning *thorny
plant eaten by donkeys.* Designated
injurious. Men compelled to root
it out within fourteen days (1959). *Full
nere desyrows.* That's how we feel, a-
part. Tiny tufts carry far by wind or stock or stream.

Jeweled, Golden, Creeping, Field, Star.

Radiance

You found the young mole skittering
near the rhododendrons
and said *I wished you'd held him because you would*
have felt how soft his fur is.

Did someone say *equation.*

Meanwhile, men are constructing immense hanging curtains made from reclaimed
tea bags. Others insist we are just recycling toxins. *In other words,*
the mailbox is the new garbage can. And the sky
still washes the dirt out to the sea.

Entire texts are circling and mirroring.

The first secret to figuring out the labyrinthine city of Fez is the rule of five,
claims a *New York Times* reporter:
5 calls to prayer. 5 pillars of Islam. 5 obligatory institutions
in each neighborhood. 5 types of design on religious buildings.

Try and tickle some part inside, you implore.

        1872 BLACKMORE *Maid of Sker v,*
; and verily she began to laugh
                        and play the blabs by kynde.
in *Spirit Pub. IX., 376,*
        I want you to give those yonder an
inward tickle
        narrow strait
                Chart S. E.
        between two
see him clinging to the bowsprit
        No sooner were we clear than

A panorama developed. The Greek word for maid: Filipineza. Hong
Kong schools: trilingual. Freegans
scavenge free-meets, flea markets. *Kynde?* Figuration of open
gaps and. Blah. Blah. What

about this emphasis on departure (we keep returning to)? Show me

scrolls of *haiga*—haiku with illustration—the one called
Man Eats Sweet Potatoes please—
and *zisha* teapots made of purple clay
(dug 10 meters down in Yixing). Yes: only in Yixing.

Equals. That is the tickle.

Acknowledgments

Thank you to the editors of the following publications, in which these poems appeared:

Barrow Street Journal: "Arachne"; "Collectio"; "Squander"; "Þ"
Colorado Review: "Aphasia"
Denver Quarterly: "Remnants"
Eccolinguistics: "Riptide"
Familia (Romania): "Eucharist Nervosa"; "Riptide"
Fence: "Radiance"
The Kenyon Review: "Alpha Protein"; "Poultice"
The Laurel Review: "Eucharist Nervosa"; "Seepage"
Literary Imagination: "Unaccounted for"
The Ocean State Review: "Old Habits"
Reconfigurations: "Erasure"
The Spoon River Poetry Review: "Æ"
Stolen Island: "Blue Moon"
Subtropic: "Border Land"
TriQuarterly: "Charcoal Suite"
Volt: "Lyms of"
The Warwick Review: "Terroir"
West Branch: "Corpse Flower"
Western Humanities Review: "Loosestrife"
Women's Studies Quarterly: "A Karstic"

A number of the poems in this book appeared in my chapbook, *Unshelter,* in 2009; my thanks to the Noemi Press editors Carmen Giménez Smith and Rosa Alcala, and to Mary Jo Bang, who selected my work for this honor.

Finally, my sincere thanks to Lynn Emanuel, who selected this book for the Barrow Street Press Poetry Prize, and to all the editors at the press, especially Robert Drummond, Mary Giaimo and Peter Covino, who steered *Vestigial* to completion with great care and attention.

Page Hill Starzinger lives in New York City, has worked as Copy Director at *Vogue*, Senior Writer at Estee Lauder, and is currently Creative Director for Copy at Aveda. Her poems have appeared or are forthcoming in *Colorado Review, Denver Quarterly, Fence, Kenyon Review, Literary Imagination, Pleiades, Volt,* and many others. Her poem, "Series #22 (white)," was chosen by Tomaz Salamun for a broadside created by The Center for Book Arts, NYC, in 2008. Her chapbook, *Unshelter,* selected by Mary Jo Bang as winner of the Noemi contest, was published in 2009. This is her first book.

Barrow Street Poetry

Gold Star Road
Richard Hoffman (2007)

Hidden Sequel
Stan Sanvel Rubin (2006)

Annus Mirabilis
Sally Ball (2005)

A Hat on the Bed
Christine Scanlon (2004)

Hiatus
Evelyn Reilly (2004)

3.14159+
Lois Hirshkowitz (2004)

Selah
Joshua Corey (2003)